Work-Life Equilibrium

Mastering Job Fulfillment and Personal Growth

Written by
Morgan E. Blake

Independently published

2024

Copyright © 2024 by Morgan E. Blake

All rights reserved.

No part of this publication may be reproduced, distributed, or transmitted in any form or by any means, including photocopying, recording, or other electronic or mechanical methods, without the prior written permission of the publisher, except in the case of brief quotations embodied in critical reviews and certain other noncommercial uses permitted by copyright law.

For permission requests, write to the publisher, addressed "Attention: Permissions Coordinator," at the address below.

info@socialized.cloud

Published by Morgan E. Blake

Book Layout ©2024 Morgan E. Blake

Cover Design ©2024 Morgan E. Blake

ISBN: 9798324967697

First Printing, 2024

Introduction

The Quest for Balance in Modern Careers

In today's fast-paced and ever-evolving job market, the pursuit of **work-life equilibrium** has become more than just a desirable attribute—it's a necessary foundation for sustainable career growth and personal well-being. This balance is not merely about managing time; it's about aligning one's career ambitions with personal values and lifestyle choices, ensuring that neither is sacrificed at the expense of the other.

The modern professional landscape presents a multitude of challenges that can disrupt this delicate balance. **Technological advancements** have blurred the lines between work hours and personal time, often extending the workday well beyond the traditional boundaries. Moreover, the rise of **global connectivity** means that many are now competing in a worldwide job market, further intensifying pressures and expectations.

In response to these challenges, the concept of work-life equilibrium has evolved. No longer is it sufficient to strive for a simple equilibrium where work and personal life are held in equal measure. Today, the focus has shifted towards a more dynamic interaction where both aspects of life enhance and complement one another. This holistic approach recognizes that a fulfilling career can significantly contribute to personal happiness, just as a rewarding personal life can bolster professional performance.

To achieve such equilibrium, it is crucial to first understand the unique pressures of modern careers. The demand for **constant availability** via smartphones and other devices can lead to a scenario where one is always "on"—a state that is unsustainable in the long run. This constant connectivity can lead to stress, burnout, and a decline in job performance, which paradoxically can damage the very career one strives to advance.

Adopting strategic practices is essential in navigating these waters. This includes setting clear boundaries between work and personal time, something that is often easier said than done. It also involves embracing flexibility in work arrangements, such as remote work or flexible hours, which can help align work responsibilities with personal needs and preferences.

Furthermore, maintaining work-life equilibrium requires a proactive approach to personal development. This encompasses continual learning and skill development, which not only enhances job performance but also fosters personal growth and satisfaction. By staying ahead in one's field and adapting to new trends, individuals can better manage career transitions and disruptions, thereby securing both their professional future and personal happiness.

Ultimately, achieving work-life equilibrium is not a one-time task, but a continuous process that adapates as one's life and career evolve. It demands regular reflection, adjustment, and sometimes, significant changes to one's work and lifestyle. It's about making informed choices and sometimes tough decisions to ensure that work enriches life, rather than detracts from it.

This introductory exploration sets the stage for the deeper discussions and strategies outlined in subsequent chapters of this book. Through a thoughtful blend of research and practical advice, *Work-Life Equilibrium: Mastering Job Fulfillment and Personal Growth* aims to equip you with the tools necessary to thrive in both your personal and professional life, fostering a sense of fulfillment that permeates all aspects of your existence. This journey is not just about surviving the modern career landscape but about thriving within it, building a life where work and personal happiness are in sync, each enhancing the value of the other.

Overview of Work-Life Equilibrium

At the core of modern career development is the concept of **work-life equilibrium**, a term that goes beyond the traditional notion of balance to describe a more fluid and personalized relationship between professional responsibilities and personal life. This holistic approach acknowledges that the integration of work and life components isn't about splitting hours evenly but about creating a synergy that enhances the quality of both.

Work-life equilibrium is predicated on the understanding that one's job and personal life are not competing interests, but complementary parts of a whole. This perspective is critical in a world where work often spills into personal time, and personal issues can affect professional performance. The aim is to configure a lifestyle where work and personal activities harmonize, leading to increased productivity at work and more enjoyment and fulfillment in life.

The pursuit of this equilibrium begins with an assessment of personal and professional goals, understanding that these objectives may shift over time. It involves evaluating what fulfillment looks like on both fronts and devising strategies to achieve it without compromising one for the other. Key to this process is the ability to adapt and respond to life's inevitable changes and challenges.

Setting Realistic Expectations

Central to achieving work-life equilibrium is setting realistic expectations for what can be accomplished within given time frames. This involves accepting that perfection is often unattainable and that good enough is sometimes sufficient. By setting achievable goals, individuals can avoid the frustration and burnout that come from striving for unrealistic standards in both work and personal life.

The Role of Flexibility

Flexibility is another cornerstone of work-life equilibrium. In today's dynamic work environment, rigid schedules and strict adherence to traditional working hours are often counterproductive. Flexibility—whether in terms of hours, location, or job duties—allows individuals to work in ways that best suit their energy levels and personal commitments. This adaptability is essential not only for managing personal responsibilities but also for accommodating the natural ebbs and flows of productive energy throughout the day.

Technology as a Tool for Equilibrium

Technology plays a dual role in work-life equilibrium. On one hand, digital tools and platforms can help manage time more effectively, facilitate remote work, and automate routine tasks. On the other hand, unchecked technology use can lead to overwork and stress. Therefore, harnessing technology to serve our needs, rather than becoming enslaved by our devices, is crucial for maintaining equilibrium.

Cultivating a Supportive Network

Achieving work-life equilibrium also depends on one's support network, which can include family, friends, colleagues, and mentors. This network can provide not only emotional support and practical help but also advice and guidance during challenging times. Cultivating strong relationships ensures that when work or personal life becomes overwhelming, there's a safety net to fall back on.

Continuous Reflection and Adjustment

Finally, maintaining work-life equilibrium requires continuous reflection and adjustment. What works well at one stage of a person's career or life may not be suitable later on. Regularly taking stock of one's current situation and making necessary adjustments is vital. This might mean changing jobs, reducing hours, or reevaluating personal goals to ensure that both work and personal life are aligned with one's current values and needs.

In the following chapters, detailed strategies and practical tips will be presented to help navigate these aspects of work-life equilibrium. Each chapter will delve deeper into the tools and mindsets needed to build a fulfilling career while enjoying a rich and rewarding personal life. By embracing the principles of work-life equilibrium, one can craft a life where career and personal success are not just possible, but are mutually reinforcing, leading to greater overall satisfaction and happiness. This is not merely about surviving the modern work landscape; it is about thriving within it, using work-life equilibrium as a foundation for lasting fulfillment.

Chapter 1: Understanding Work-Life Balance

Defining Work-Life Equilibrium

As we delve deeper into the concept of work-life equilibrium, it is crucial to first establish a clear definition of what this term really encompasses. **Work-life equilibrium** is not merely about balancing a scale between professional duties and personal activities; rather, it represents a more nuanced approach to integrating all aspects of one's life in a way that allows each part to thrive and support the other.

Equilibrium implies a coexistence where the elements do not compete but complement and enhance one another. In the context of work and life, this means creating an environment where professional achievements and personal satisfaction are not at odds but are interwoven to create a richer, more fulfilling experience. It's about finding synergy rather than sacrificing one aspect for the sake of the other.

The Fluidity of Equilibrium

One of the key characteristics of work-life equilibrium is its **fluidity**. Unlike the static notion of balance, which suggests a rigid, equal distribution, equilibrium allows for flexibility and change over time. It recognizes that life's demands are not constant; they ebb and flow depending on various factors including career phases, personal milestones, and external pressures. What constitutes equilibrium today may need reevaluation tomorrow as circumstances change.

Personalization of Equilibrium

Work-life equilibrium is deeply personal and varies widely from one individual to another. What feels harmonious for one person might feel chaotic or imbalanced to another. For example, a young entrepreneur might find equilibrium in merging their work and personal life, often working late but taking breaks throughout the day for personal activities. In contrast, a parent might prefer distinct boundaries between work hours and family time to ensure quality attention to both areas.

Achieving Work-Life Equilibrium

Achieving this equilibrium begins with self-awareness. It requires understanding one's own priorities, values, and limits. This understanding forms the basis for setting boundaries and making choices that align with one's overall life goals. It also involves communication—articulating needs and expectations to employers, colleagues, and family members to negotiate the necessary space and flexibility.

Tools and Strategies

Employing specific tools and strategies can facilitate work-life equilibrium. These might include:

- **Effective Time Management**: Utilizing tools and techniques to manage one's time efficiently not only boosts productivity but also creates space for personal pursuits and relaxation.

- **Technological Aids**: Leveraging technology to automate routine tasks can free up time for more meaningful work and interaction with loved ones.

- **Boundary Setting**: Learning to say no and setting clear boundaries around work hours and personal time can help maintain the integrity of one's personal space and work commitments.

The Role of Employers

Employers also play a significant role in supporting work-life equilibrium. Companies that cultivate a culture of flexibility, offer support for personal development, and recognize the individual needs of their employees can greatly enhance their team's overall equilibrium and satisfaction. Practices such as flexible working hours, remote work options, and support for mental health are becoming increasingly important in modern workplaces.

Conclusion on Defining Work-Life Equilibrium

Ultimately, defining work-life equilibrium is about recognizing that the pursuit of a fulfilled and contented life is a holistic endeavor. It is not about compartmentalizing life into work and personal categories but about weaving these aspects together in a way that supports overall well-being. This book aims to explore these dimensions, offering insights and strategies that help readers construct their own version of equilibrium, tailored to their unique life circumstances. By understanding and implementing the principles of work-life equilibrium, individuals can aspire to not just manage but thrive in all areas of their lives, enhancing both their professional achievements and personal satisfaction. This approach is not merely about navigating the complexities of modern employment; it's about transforming them into opportunities for a richer, more vibrant life.

The Evolution of Work Demands and Personal Life

To fully appreciate the nuances of work-life equilibrium, it is essential to examine how both work demands and personal life expectations have evolved over the decades. This evolution has been influenced by a myriad of factors, including technological advancements, shifts in societal values, and changes in the global economy. These dynamics have reshaped what it means to work and live, altering our approaches to balancing the two.

The Historical Context

In the mid-20th century, the typical work model was fairly rigid, characterized by fixed hours and often a clear separation between work and home life. This was the era of the 9-to-5 job, primarily in industrial or administrative settings, where work was something distinct from personal or family life. However, as the service sector expanded and the information age took hold, these boundaries began to blur.

Technological Impact

The advent of personal computing and the internet revolutionized the workplace. By the late 20th century, email and digital communication began to challenge the traditional workday, introducing new flexibility but also new expectations of availability. This trend only accelerated with the proliferation of smartphones and cloud computing, leading to a scenario where employees could—and often were expected to—work from anywhere and at any time.

Societal Shifts

Concurrently, societal attitudes toward work and personal life also began to shift. There was a growing recognition of the importance of work-life balance as essential to health and well-being. This was paralleled by changes in gender roles, with more dual-career couples and increasing demands for equitable sharing of domestic responsibilities. These changes prompted a reevaluation of what individuals expected from their employers in terms of flexibility and support.

The Millennial Influence

Millennials entering the workforce brought with them different priorities, such as the desire for meaningful and fulfilling work, greater flexibility, and a better balance between their professional and personal lives. This generational shift has pressured organizations to rethink their work cultures and policies, leading to more progressive initiatives like unlimited vacation days, flexible working conditions, and wellness programs.

Globalization and Economic Shifts

Globalization has further complicated the work-life equation. Companies operate across multiple time zones, and competition has increased from a global talent pool. Economic shifts, including recessions and booms, have also played a role in shaping employment trends, sometimes straining work-life dynamics as individuals work longer hours or multiple jobs to meet economic challenges.

The COVID-19 Pandemic

The recent global pandemic has been a pivotal influence, dramatically accelerating trends towards remote work and proving that many jobs can be performed effectively outside of traditional office settings. This shift has provided a unique opportunity to reimagine work-life equilibrium, with many individuals and companies seeing the benefits of flexible work models for the first time.

Looking Ahead

As we move forward, it is likely that work and personal life will continue to integrate in increasingly complex ways. The challenge will be to manage this integration in a manner that enhances well-being and productivity without leading to burnout. This will require not only adaptive strategies from individuals but also supportive policies from employers who recognize the changing dynamics of the modern workforce.

In this context, understanding the historical and ongoing evolution of work demands and personal life is more than an academic exercise—it's a critical foundation for building strategies that support sustainable work-life equilibrium. As we explore these strategies further, the goal will be to provide actionable insights that can be adapted to diverse life scenarios, helping individuals navigate a world where the lines between work and personal life are not just blurred but continuously shifting. This exploration aims not just to adapt to these changes but to actively shape them in ways that enrich both our careers and our personal lives.

Chapter 2: The Psychology of Work Satisfaction

What Makes a Job Fulfilling?

In the pursuit of career satisfaction, the question of what makes a job fulfilling stands as a cornerstone of personal and professional development. Fulfillment at work transcends the basic metrics of success such as salary, position, or status. It digs deeper into the psychological and emotional engagement that one feels towards their occupation. Understanding these facets is essential for cultivating a work environment where one not only survives but thrives.

The Elements of Job Fulfillment

Purpose and Meaning: Central to job fulfillment is the feeling that one's work has purpose and meaning. This is the sense that the work contributes to something larger than oneself, aligning with personal values and making a positive impact on the world. When individuals see the fruits of their labor contributing to societal good or aligning with their personal values, their day-to-day tasks gain an enriched sense of importance and satisfaction.

Autonomy: The ability to make decisions and have control over one's work processes is a significant driver of job fulfillment. Autonomy empowers individuals, fostering a sense of ownership and responsibility. It allows for creativity and personal growth, as employees feel trusted to shape their work environment and methods.

Mastery and Competence: A fulfilling job is one that challenges an individual but also allows for continuous growth and learning. The opportunity to master new skills and improve one's competencies not only makes one more proficient but also more engaged and interested in their work. This sense of progress is deeply satisfying and contributes to long-term career happiness.

Recognition and Appreciation: Feeling recognized and appreciated for one's efforts is a fundamental human need. In the workplace, this translates into feedback and rewards that acknowledge an employee's contributions. Recognition from peers and supervisors can reinforce a positive self-image and motivate further effort and engagement.

Relationships and Social Support: The relationships cultivated in the workplace play a crucial role in job fulfillment. A supportive work environment characterized by trust, respect, and camaraderie can enhance job satisfaction by making daily interactions more enjoyable and providing a network of support during challenging times.

Work-Life Equilibrium: As the central theme of this book, work-life equilibrium is integral to job fulfillment. A job that allows for a healthy balance between professional responsibilities and personal life leads to reduced stress and increased overall happiness. Employers who support and facilitate this balance contribute significantly to the fulfillment of their employees.

Personal Alignment and Job Fit

Beyond these elements, job fulfillment is also deeply personal and varies widely among individuals. What fulfills one person might not satisfy another. This variation is often due to differences in personality, life stage, and personal circumstances. Therefore, understanding oneself—knowing one's passions, values, and desired lifestyle—is critical when seeking or shaping a fulfilling job.

Creating Fulfillment in Any Job

While some jobs may naturally align more closely with these criteria, it is possible to find fulfillment in a wide range of professions. Initiatives can be taken by individuals to enhance their job satisfaction such as seeking projects that align with personal values, advocating for autonomy in their roles, or engaging in continuous learning to advance their skills.

Additionally, fostering a positive workplace culture and building strong relationships at work can significantly enhance how fulfilling one finds their job. Even in less-than-ideal job circumstances, focusing on elements of work that do align with personal values and strengths can increase satisfaction.

The Role of Employers in Enhancing Job Fulfillment

Employers play a crucial role in this equation. By creating environments that prioritize these aspects of job fulfillment—purpose, autonomy, mastery, recognition, and support—they can enhance the satisfaction and productivity of their workforce. Progressive workplace policies that promote flexibility, provide opportunities for personal development, and recognize and reward contributions can help cultivate a culture of fulfillment.

In conclusion, job fulfillment is multifaceted and deeply personal. It is influenced by both the intrinsic characteristics of the job and the extrinsic environment provided by employers. As we continue to navigate the complexities of the modern workforce, understanding these dynamics is more crucial than ever. It allows both individuals and organizations to strive towards creating work situations that are not only productive but deeply fulfilling. By fostering an environment where employees find purpose, autonomy, mastery, recognition, and support, we pave the way for more satisfying and sustainable careers. This focus on fulfillment is essential for anyone looking to transform their work life into a source of joy and satisfaction.

The Role of Motivation and Engagement

Delving into the psychology of work satisfaction, it becomes evident that **motivation and engagement** are pivotal elements that profoundly influence job fulfillment and overall productivity. Understanding these concepts not only enhances individual careers but also bolsters the dynamics within teams and organizations.

Understanding Motivation

Motivation in the workplace stems from a combination of intrinsic and extrinsic factors. **Intrinsic motivation** is driven by internal rewards, such as personal satisfaction, a sense of achievement, or the joy of doing something that aligns with one's passions and values. It is the motivation that compels an individual to act for the sake of the activity itself rather than for some separable consequence. On the other hand, **extrinsic motivation** involves performing a task in order to attain some separable outcome, which could include financial rewards, recognition, or promotion.

The balance between these two types of motivation can significantly affect how individuals perceive their roles and responsibilities within a job. When intrinsic motivation dominates, employees are likely to experience higher job satisfaction, exhibit greater creativity, and maintain sustained productivity levels. Conversely, while extrinsic motivators are important, over-reliance on them can lead to decreased motivation once the rewards stop.

The Spectrum of Engagement

Employee engagement, closely tied to motivation, refers to the emotional commitment an employee has to their organization and its goals. This commitment means engaged employees genuinely care about their work and their company. They don't work just for a paycheck, or just for the next promotion, but work on behalf of the organization's goals. When employees are engaged, they are more likely to be productive and remain with their employer.

There are typically three levels of engagement found in the workplace:

1. **Engaged**: Employees who are enthusiastic about their work and take positive action to further the organization's reputation and interests.

2. **Not Engaged**: Employees who are essentially 'checked out', putting time but not energy or passion into their work.

3. **Actively Disengaged**: Employees who aren't just unhappy at work; they are resentful that their needs aren't being met and are acting out their unhappiness.

The goal for any organization should be to maximize the number of engaged employees while minimizing and managing those who are not engaged or actively disengaged.

Fostering Motivation and Engagement

Creating a work environment that fosters motivation and engagement requires several strategic actions:

- **Meaningful Work**: Ensure that work tasks are meaningful to employees and aligned with their values. This alignment boosts intrinsic motivation.

- **Recognition and Rewards**: Implement a recognition system that acknowledges both small achievements and big wins. Tailor rewards to meet the diverse needs and desires of employees.

- **Professional Growth**: Provide opportunities for employees to learn new skills or advance their knowledge in areas of interest. Career development is a powerful motivator.

- **Autonomy and Responsibility**: Empower employees by providing them with autonomy in their tasks and responsibilities. This empowerment enhances their intrinsic motivation and satisfaction with their work.

- **Healthy Work Culture**: Cultivate a supportive and inclusive work culture that encourages collaboration and open communication. A positive environment nurtures engagement.

The Impact of Motivation and Engagement

The benefits of high motivation and engagement are substantial. They lead to better performance, lower turnover, fewer absences, and higher profitability. Moreover, they contribute to a positive organizational reputation, attracting top talent in competitive job markets.

Ultimately, the key to sustaining motivation and engagement lies in understanding and addressing the unique drivers for each individual within an organization. This personalized approach ensures that employees not only come to work but are excited about what they do and are committed to the organization's success.

This exploration into the role of motivation and engagement is fundamental to mastering job fulfillment and achieving work-life equilibrium. By fostering an environment where motivation is nurtured and engagement is the norm, both individuals and organizations can reach their full potential, turning everyday tasks into sources of joy and satisfaction. This isn't just about making people work harder; it's about making work more fulfilling, ensuring that each day brings opportunities for growth and happiness.

Chapter 3: Strategies for Achieving Work-Life Equilibrium

Prioritizing Tasks and Responsibilities

In the journey toward achieving work-life equilibrium, the ability to effectively prioritize tasks and responsibilities emerges as a pivotal skill. This skill not only enhances professional productivity but also ensures that personal life receives the attention it deserves, fostering a fulfilling and balanced lifestyle.

Understanding the Value of Prioritization

Prioritization is the art of ranking tasks based on their importance and urgency, ensuring that the most critical activities receive the attention needed before others. Effective prioritization not only aids in meeting deadlines and achieving goals but also reduces stress, as it helps clear the clutter of less significant tasks that can often distract from what truly matters.

The Eisenhower Matrix: A Tool for Prioritization

One of the most effective tools for prioritization is the **Eisenhower Matrix**, developed by Dwight D. Eisenhower. This matrix divides tasks into four quadrants based on their urgency and importance:

- **Quadrant 1: Important and Urgent** — Tasks that require immediate attention.

- **Quadrant 2: Important but Not Urgent** — Tasks that are important but do not require immediate action.

- **Quadrant 3: Not Important but Urgent** — Tasks that require immediate attention but are not necessarily important.

- **Quadrant 4: Not Important and Not Urgent** — Tasks that are neither urgent nor important.

Focusing on Quadrant 2 tasks (Important but Not Urgent) is key to strategic planning and long-term success, as these are often linked to achieving one's broader goals.

Strategies for Effective Task Prioritization

- **Clear Goal Setting**: Begin by clearly defining both short-term and long-term goals. Understanding these goals helps in aligning tasks in order of their contribution towards these objectives.

- **Daily Planning**: Utilize the beginning of each day to prioritize tasks. This can involve listing daily tasks and applying the Eisenhower Matrix to identify where each task fits.

- **Technology and Tools**: Leverage technology such as task management apps and digital calendars. Tools like Asana, Trello, and Google Calendar can aid in visualizing tasks' priority and deadlines.

- **Delegation**: Recognize tasks that can be delegated to others. Delegation is not just a way to lighten one's load but also an opportunity to empower team members, helping them grow and develop new skills.

The Role of Flexibility in Prioritization

While it is essential to have a plan, it is equally important to maintain flexibility. The workday can often bring unexpected challenges or opportunities; hence, being flexible allows for adjustments without significant disruptions. This adaptability is crucial in maintaining a balanced approach to both professional and personal commitments.

Maintaining a Long-term Perspective

In the pursuit of work-life equilibrium, prioritization should not be seen as a daily checklist but rather as part of a larger strategy aimed at fulfilling life goals. This perspective ensures that daily tasks are steps towards larger achievements and personal growth.

The Psychological Benefits of Prioritization

Prioritizing effectively reduces anxiety and can increase one's sense of control and competence. It alleviates the feeling of being overwhelmed and supports a more focused and calm approach to both work and personal life challenges.

Concluding Reflections on Prioritization

Mastering the skill of prioritization is essential for anyone aiming to achieve a balanced and productive life. It allows for the juggling of numerous responsibilities while ensuring that each action is a stepping stone towards greater objectives. By cultivating effective prioritization habits, individuals can ensure that their professional tasks are aligned with personal goals and values, thus enhancing overall life satisfaction.

Embracing this structured approach to handling responsibilities ensures that both career aspirations and personal well-being are not just dreamt about but actively pursued. The journey towards work-life equilibrium is thus marked not by a frantic pace but by a deliberate and thoughtful progression towards fulfillment and success. This pursuit is not merely about managing time but about managing life's opportunities and challenges in a way that aligns with one's deepest aspirations and values.

Effective Time Management Techniques

In the quest for work-life equilibrium, effective time management emerges as a critical skill, essential for maximizing productivity while ensuring personal well-being. Mastering this skill involves not just managing one's time but optimizing it in a way that aligns with personal and professional goals, making each day more productive and fulfilling.

Understanding Time Management

Time management is the process of organizing and planning how to divide your time between specific activities. Good time management enables you to work smarter – not harder – so that you get more done in less time, even when time is tight and pressures are high. Failing to manage your time damages your effectiveness and causes stress.

Techniques for Enhancing Time Efficiency

1. Goal Setting: Begin with clear, actionable goals. Goals should be SMART: Specific, Measurable, Achievable, Relevant, and Time-bound. By defining these, you create a roadmap for your day-to-day activities that guide your actions to be both purposeful and results-focused.

2. Prioritization: As previously discussed, using tools like the Eisenhower Box can help identify what tasks require immediate attention and which ones could be scheduled for later or delegated. Prioritizing tasks ensures that you spend your time and energy on activities that align closely with your overall objectives.

3. The Pomodoro Technique: This involves working in blocks of time, typically 25 minutes long, followed by a 5-minute break. These intervals are referred to as 'Pomodoros'. After four Pomodoros, you take a longer break of about 15 to 20 minutes. This technique helps maintain high levels of concentration and staves off fatigue.

4. Time Blocking: Allocate specific blocks of time on your calendar for different activities. This not only includes work-related tasks but also personal time for breaks, exercise, and family. Time blocking helps to create a balanced schedule that dedicates space to varied activities, enhancing focus during work periods and ensuring time for relaxation and personal growth.

5. Delegation and Outsourcing: Understand which tasks require your personal attention and which can be handled by others. Effective delegation involves assigning the right tasks to the right people. This not only frees up your time but also empowers others by entrusting them with more responsibilities.

6. Setting Boundaries: Firm boundaries will protect your time from external interruptions. This might mean having specific hours where you are unavailable for meetings or calls, or it could involve setting up an office space that limits interruptions from family members during work hours.

7. Using Technology Wisely: Leverage technology to save time. This can include using project management tools, automating repetitive tasks, or employing AI assistants for scheduling. However, it's also crucial to manage technology use to prevent it from becoming a distraction—like setting limits on social media use during work hours.

The Importance of Flexibility

While structure is essential in time management, flexibility is equally important. Life is unpredictable, and rigid schedules can sometimes add unnecessary pressure. Being flexible allows you to adapt to changes without significant stress, adjusting your plan as needed while still focusing on your priorities.

Reflective Practice

End each day with a brief reflection on what was accomplished and what could be improved. This helps in recognizing the productivity strategies that are working and those that need adjustment. Reflection fosters a mindset of continuous improvement, essential for effective time management.

Conclusion on Time Management

Effective time management is not just about filling every minute of the day with tasks but about finding a rhythm that allows for the ebb and flow of work and leisure, ultimately supporting your quest for work-life equilibrium. By implementing these techniques, you set the stage for days that are not only productive but also balanced and fulfilling. Remember, the goal is to make time work for you, not against you, turning it into a tool for achieving both your career aspirations and personal contentment. This way, each moment becomes a step towards a more satisfied, balanced life.

Chapter 4: The Impact of Workplace Culture

How Organizational Culture Influences Balance

Exploring the profound impact organizational culture has on achieving work-life equilibrium unveils a critical aspect of modern employment dynamics. An organization's culture encompasses the shared values, beliefs, and practices that shape the behavior and decision-making within a company. This culture can profoundly influence an employee's ability to find balance between professional commitments and personal life.

Defining Organizational Culture

Organizational culture is the framework within which members of an organization interact with each other and with the outside environment. It includes leadership styles, communication patterns, internal policies, and the company's mission and values. How these elements are aligned and practiced influences the overall atmosphere of the workplace and the well-being of its employees.

The Role of Leadership in Shaping Culture

Leaders play a pivotal role in setting the tone of the organizational culture. Their approach to management, their behavior, and how they handle stress and work-life balance themselves often set a model for other employees. Leaders who prioritize their own and their employees' work-life equilibrium tend to create an environment where such balance is achievable and valued.

Communication and Transparency

Open and honest communication is a cornerstone of a supportive organizational culture. When employees feel they can openly discuss their needs regarding flexibility or personal obligations without fear of repercussions, they are more likely to feel satisfied and less stressed. Transparency from management about company goals, changes, and expectations can also reduce uncertainties that might otherwise lead to job stress and work-life conflict.

Policies that Promote Work-Life Equilibrium

Organizational policies play a significant role in facilitating work-life balance. These may include:

- **Flexible working hours** and the possibility of remote work, allowing employees to adjust their work schedules to better fit personal responsibilities.

- **Paid time off** policies that encourage employees to take vacations and personal days to rest and rejuvenate.
- **Parental leave** policies that support both mothers and fathers, recognizing the importance of involvement in family life.
- **Employee assistance programs** that offer counseling and support for personal or work-related issues.

Creating a Supportive Environment

A culture that supports work-life balance also promotes an environment of support among coworkers. This involves:

- Team collaboration and support mechanisms that allow employees to help each other balance workload efficiently.
- Recognition of personal milestones and support during personal challenges, which can foster a sense of community and mutual respect.
- Encouragement of social interactions outside of work tasks, which can strengthen bonds and improve teamwork.

Impact on Employee Retention and Attraction

Organizations with cultures that promote work-life balance are more likely to retain their employees. In today's job market, where many have options, employees are likely to gravitate towards and stay longer with employers who support their pursuit of a balanced life. Moreover, such cultures attract top talent who value personal well-being alongside career growth.

Case Studies: Learning from the Best

Consider the examples of companies renowned for their supportive cultures, such as Google and Netflix, which offer extensive work-life balance policies ranging from flexible working conditions to mental health support programs. These companies not only report higher employee satisfaction but also enjoy increased productivity and creativity among their workforce.

Reflecting on Organizational Culture and Its Influence

In essence, the culture of an organization is not just about the work environment but about fostering a holistic approach to employee well-being. It reflects a philosophy that when employees are well-cared-for, they perform better and contribute more effectively to the organization's goals. This philosophy ultimately serves as the bedrock for sustainable business success.

Embracing a culture that promotes work-life equilibrium requires a commitment from all levels of an organization, particularly from top leadership. By prioritizing these values, organizations not only enhance their employees' quality of life but also position themselves as leaders in a competitive global marketplace, where the best talent thrives in environments that respect and support their life beyond work. This holistic approach is not merely a perk but a crucial element in the future of work, where balance and well-being are key to unlocking true potential.

Case Studies: Companies Excelling in Employee Satisfaction

In this exploration of companies that are leaders in fostering employee satisfaction, we'll delve into specific case studies that exemplify how embracing innovative practices and nurturing a positive organizational culture can significantly enhance work-life equilibrium. These companies not only excel in creating environments where employees thrive but also demonstrate the profound impact of such practices on overall business success.

Google: Prioritizing Innovation and Well-being

Google has long been recognized for its revolutionary approach to workplace culture, heavily emphasizing both employee well-being and continuous innovation. The tech giant's corporate ethos is based on the belief that work should be challenging but the challenge should be fun. At Google, the office is not just a place to work but a place to live a fulfilling life during work hours. Facilities like on-site healthcare, gyms, laundry services, and access to a variety of wellness resources underscore its commitment to employee well-being.

Google's approach extends beyond physical benefits to include substantial support for personal and professional development. Programs like '20% Time'—where employees can spend 20% of their work time on projects they are passionate about—foster a sense of ownership and satisfaction. This autonomy to pursue creative projects has not only led to significant product developments but has also kept motivation and job satisfaction levels high.

Netflix: Flexibility and Responsibility

Netflix's culture is famously encapsulated by its philosophy of 'Freedom and Responsibility.' The company offers one of the most flexible working environments in the tech industry, which includes unlimited vacation days and a telecommuting option. Such policies are predicated on trust—Netflix trusts its employees to make the best decisions regarding their time and workload management.

Moreover, Netflix's commitment to transparency and communication is evident in its routine '360-degree reviews,' where employees receive constructive feedback from peers, subordinates, and superiors alike. This culture of candid feedback ensures problems are addressed promptly and that the organization's goals are continuously aligned with employee growth and satisfaction.

Patagonia: Integrating Values and Work

Patagonia stands out for its commitment to environmental sustainability and how it integrates this value into its corporate culture. The company's dedication to 'cause no unnecessary harm' is not just external but applies internally as well. Patagonia offers on-site childcare and encourages employees to participate in environmental initiatives during work hours.

This integration of corporate values with daily operations engenders a deep sense of purpose and loyalty among employees, many of whom are drawn to the company for its environmental stance. By aligning its operational practices with its ethical values, Patagonia ensures that employees do not have to compromise their personal ideals for their professional lives, enhancing overall job satisfaction.

SAS: Emphasizing Employee Support and Balance

SAS Institute has consistently been ranked as one of the top companies to work for, largely due to its focus on creating a supportive work environment. The company offers a plethora of benefits designed to enhance life both inside and outside of work, including subsidized childcare, healthcare centers, and a work environment that encourages a reasonable work-life balance.

SAS's philosophy is that happy, healthy employees create a positive and productive work environment. This belief is manifested in their low employee turnover rates and high job satisfaction scores, proving that a focus on comprehensive employee well-being directly correlates with enhanced productivity and loyalty.

Reflecting on These Examples

These companies demonstrate that when organizations invest in the well-being of their employees and align corporate policies with the values and needs of their workforce, they not only enhance employee satisfaction but also improve their overall business performance. Each case study provides a unique perspective on how adopting different strategies—be it through innovative benefits, flexibility, value integration, or supportive environments—can lead to successful outcomes in both employee satisfaction and business excellence.

Exploring these examples offers valuable insights into how diverse strategies and policies can be effectively implemented to support employees' needs, leading to a more motivated, engaged, and productive workforce. By considering these successful models, other organizations can be inspired to reevaluate and possibly revamp their own practices to better support their employees, ultimately fostering a workplace where both the company and its people can thrive together.

Chapter 5: Tools and Technologies for Modern Job Hunters

Leveraging Job Hunting Tools to Find the Right Fit

In today's complex and ever-evolving job market, effectively navigating the vast array of opportunities requires more than just diligence and perseverance. It demands strategic utilization of varied job hunting tools designed to not only discover opportunities but also to match one's unique skills and career aspirations with the right employer. Understanding how to leverage these tools can significantly enhance your ability to find a job that not only meets your professional needs but also aligns with your personal life, fostering true work-life equilibrium.

Comprehensive Understanding of Available Tools

Online Job Portals: Websites like Indeed, Glassdoor, and LinkedIn are at the forefront of online job hunting. They offer extensive databases of job listings and company reviews, allowing you to filter searches by industry, job title, location, and expected salary. These platforms also provide valuable insights into company cultures and employee reviews, which can be pivotal in determining if an organization aligns with your personal and professional values.

Resume Building Software: Crafting a compelling resume is crucial in catching the attention of potential employers. Tools like Canva and Zety offer user-friendly resume templates that are both visually appealing and structured to highlight your strongest attributes effectively. They help ensure your resume is not only comprehensive but also tailored to the specific nuances and requirements of jobs you are applying for.

Professional Networking Platforms: LinkedIn, beyond just job listings, serves as a vital networking tool. It allows you to connect with industry professionals and participate in groups and discussions that can increase your visibility and credibility within your field. Regular interaction and networking can lead to job referrals and opportunities that are often not advertised publicly.

Career Development Blogs and Podcasts: Staying updated with the latest industry trends and advice is essential. Blogs like "Ask a Manager" or podcasts such as "The Tim Ferriss Show" can provide ongoing insights and strategies for job hunting and career development, which are invaluable in making informed decisions about your career path.

Interview Preparation Tools: Companies like Big Interview offer coaching and mock interviews that can significantly bolster your confidence and improve your performance in actual job interviews. These tools provide feedback from career coaches and use AI-driven algorithms to analyze your responses, helping refine your interview skills.

Strategic Application of These Tools

Using these tools effectively involves more than just passive browsing. It requires a strategic and active approach:

1. **Set Clear Goals**: Know what you want in terms of industry, job role, and work-life balance. Setting clear goals helps in using these tools more effectively to find opportunities that align with your aspirations.

2. **Customize Applications**: Tailor your resume and cover letters for each application based on insights gained from job portals and company reviews. Customization shows potential employers your genuine interest and fit for the position.

3. **Engage Actively on Networking Sites**: Don't just create profiles; engage with others, share relevant content, and participate in discussions. This active engagement increases

your visibility and portrays you as a proactive industry participant.

4. **Continuous Learning**: Utilize blogs and podcasts not just during job searches but as a part of your ongoing professional development. This continuous learning helps you stay relevant and knowledgeable about your industry, making you a more attractive candidate.

Reflecting on the Impact

The effective use of these tools not only streamlines the job search process but also significantly increases the chances of finding a job that is a perfect fit for your professional skills and personal life goals. The right fit is crucial not just for job satisfaction but for long-term career success and personal fulfillment.

In conclusion, as you navigate the waters of modern employment, remember that the tools at your disposal are numerous and varied. By strategically leveraging these resources, you equip yourself with the necessary skills and knowledge to not only find a job but to find the right job where you can thrive both professionally and personally. This approach ensures that your career path is not just a series of jobs but a meaningful journey aligned with your deepest values and aspirations.

Online Platforms and Networking Strategies

Navigating the modern job market requires more than just a polished resume and sharp interview skills; it demands a proactive approach to leveraging online platforms and implementing effective networking strategies. These digital arenas not only facilitate connections but also open doors to opportunities that might otherwise remain inaccessible. In this era, understanding and utilizing these tools is crucial for career advancement and personal growth.

Harnessing the Power of Professional Networking Sites

LinkedIn: The cornerstone of professional networking online, LinkedIn offers a plethora of opportunities for career development. It is not just a platform for job seekers; it serves as a professional community where you can share insights, join industry-specific groups, and engage with content relevant to your field. The key to leveraging LinkedIn effectively is an active presence:

- **Optimize Your Profile**: Ensure your profile is complete and up-to-date, with a professional photo, detailed work history, and a compelling summary that highlights your skills and career aspirations.

- **Publish Content**: Regularly share and write articles that reflect your professional interests and expertise. This establishes your reputation as a knowledgeable and engaged industry participant.
- **Network Actively**: Connect with colleagues, industry leaders, and peers. Regularly comment on posts and participate in discussions to increase your visibility.

Twitter and Other Social Media: While LinkedIn is tailored for professional networking, platforms like Twitter also offer valuable opportunities for engagement. Follow leaders and influencers in your field, contribute to relevant conversations, and use hashtags to join broader industry discussions. Platforms like Facebook and Instagram can also be utilized to follow companies and join groups that offer job alerts and career advice.

Utilizing Job Search Engines and Company Websites

Job Search Engines: Websites like Indeed, Glassdoor, and Monster provide not just job listings but also company reviews, salary benchmarks, and interview tips. To maximize these tools:

- **Set Up Job Alerts**: Customize alerts to receive notifications about new postings that match your specified criteria, ensuring you never miss an opportunity.

- **Research Employers**: Before applying, research potential employers thoroughly to understand their culture, employee satisfaction, and financial health, which are all pivotal in determining if they are a good fit for your career goals.

Company Career Pages: Often, the best opportunities are found directly on a company's career page where they might list jobs not posted elsewhere. Bookmark the careers pages of companies you are interested in and check back regularly.

Engaging in Industry Forums and Webinars

Participation in industry-specific forums and attending webinars can significantly enhance your knowledge and expose you to new opportunities. Platforms like Reddit have industry-specific subreddits where professionals discuss the latest trends, challenges, and opportunities. Webinars, often free, provide insights from industry leaders and can be a great way to learn directly from experts and ask questions in real-time.

Building and Maintaining Your Digital Persona

Consistency Across Platforms: Ensure that your professional persona is consistent across all platforms. This includes using the same professional photo, job title, and professional summary, which helps in building a recognizable personal brand.

Digital Etiquette: Networking online also requires a sense of digital etiquette. Be professional in all interactions, respect people's time, and always follow up with new contacts with a thank you message or note that acknowledges the connection.

Reflecting on the Role of Digital Tools in Modern Networking

The integration of these online platforms and networking strategies into your career development plan can not only increase your chances of finding the right job but also help in building a sustainable career path. These tools offer powerful ways to showcase your skills, learn from others, and stay connected with the pulse of your industry.

In conclusion, mastering these digital tools and strategies is not just about keeping up with the times but about actively shaping your career trajectory. By engaging with these platforms thoughtfully and consistently, you open up a world of opportunities that can lead to meaningful employment and personal fulfillment. This proactive approach is essential in navigating the complex landscape of modern employment, ensuring you remain a competitive, well-connected, and informed professional ready to take on the challenges and opportunities that come your way.

Chapter 6: Personal Development for Career Advancement

Skills Building for Today and Tomorrow

In the dynamic landscape of modern employment, continuous skill development is not just advantageous—it's essential. As we navigate through changing job markets and evolving industry standards, the ability to adapt through ongoing learning stands as a cornerstone of not only career resilience but also personal growth and satisfaction. Understanding how to effectively build and refine your skills ensures that you remain competitive and relevant, irrespective of the economic tides.

The Importance of Skill Development

Skill development goes beyond mere professional requirement; it is a fundamental component of personal empowerment and job satisfaction. As you enhance your skills, you not only increase your employability but also improve your capacity to make meaningful contributions to your work, leading to greater fulfillment and confidence in your professional role.

Identifying Key Areas for Skill Enhancement

The first step in skill development is identifying the skills that are most relevant to your career aspirations and current industry trends. This requires a dual approach:

- **Industry Analysis**: Stay informed about the latest trends in your field. What skills are most in demand? Are there emerging areas that interest you?
- **Self-Assessment**: Evaluate your current skill set. Where are the gaps? Which skills would most likely impact your career advancement and personal satisfaction?

Strategies for Effective Skill Building

Once key areas for development have been identified, the following strategies can help you effectively build these skills:

1. Formal Education and Training: Enroll in relevant courses, workshops, and seminars. Institutions and online platforms offer a range of programs designed to enhance specific skills. For instance, platforms like Coursera, Udemy, and edX provide courses in everything from data science to project management and soft skills like leadership.

2. On-the-Job Training: Seek opportunities within your current role to expand your skill set. This could be through new projects, cross-departmental collaborations, or by taking on more challenging assignments that push you out of your comfort zone.

3. Mentoring and Coaching: Engage with mentors or coaches who can provide guidance, feedback, and insights based on their experiences. This can accelerate your learning and help you navigate the complexities of your industry with greater ease.

4. Networking: Engage actively in professional networks related to your field. Networking can provide you with insights into how others are navigating their career paths and what skills they find most valuable.

5. Self-Directed Learning: Make use of online resources to self-teach. Independent learning initiatives demonstrate your commitment to personal growth and can be tailored to fit your specific learning pace and interests.

Incorporating Technology in Skill Development

Leverage technology to make learning more accessible and efficient. Many organizations offer virtual learning platforms that are designed to fit into a busy schedule. Additionally, apps and tools can provide interactive learning experiences that reinforce new skills through practical application.

Reflective Practice and Continuous Feedback

As you develop new skills, it's important to engage in reflective practice—take time to reflect on what you've learned and how you can apply it. Seek feedback from peers, supervisors, or mentors to gauge your progress and identify areas for further improvement.

Conclusion on Skills Building

In conclusion, building skills for today and tomorrow is about creating a pathway for continuous growth that aligns with your career aspirations and personal values. It is about becoming a lifelong learner who not only adapts to change but thrives in it. By investing in your skills, you not only enhance your career prospects but also contribute to a fulfilling life where growth and learning are integral to your personal and professional identity. This approach not only prepares you for the future of work but also ensures you remain passionate and engaged in your career journey, continuously finding equilibrium between your personal aspirations and professional achievements.

The Importance of Continuous Learning

In the rapidly changing landscape of today's job market, continuous learning emerges not merely as a route to career advancement but as a necessity for staying relevant and effective in any professional role. It encompasses an ongoing commitment to expanding your knowledge and skills, adapting to new technologies, and understanding evolving industry trends. This commitment is essential for maintaining work-life equilibrium as it ensures that your professional life remains fulfilling and aligned with your personal growth and evolving career aspirations.

Why Continuous Learning Is Crucial

Adapting to Technological Advances: As technology reshapes industries at an unprecedented rate, the demand for new skills escalates. Continuous learning enables you to keep pace with technological advancements, whether it's mastering new software, understanding emerging industry standards, or adapting to new business models. This adaptability is crucial not only for job security but also for seizing opportunities to advance or pivot within your career.

Enhancing Employability: In a competitive job market, those who consistently upgrade their skills set themselves apart. Continuous learning enhances your employability and opens doors to new opportunities that might require more advanced or diverse skill sets. It allows you to navigate career transitions more smoothly and with greater confidence.

Fostering Innovation and Creativity: Regular exposure to new ideas and knowledge fosters creativity. By engaging in continuous learning, you refresh your perspective and stimulate your mind, which can lead to innovation within your role or projects. This not only contributes to job satisfaction but also enhances your value as an employee who can bring fresh ideas and solutions to the table.

Building Professional Confidence and Competence: Learning new skills and deepening your knowledge can significantly boost your professional confidence. This confidence is key to taking initiative, voicing ideas, and leading projects. Furthermore, increased competence allows you to handle complex challenges more effectively, reducing stress and enhancing overall job satisfaction.

How to Engage in Continuous Learning

Formal Education and Certifications: Pursuing formal education such as advanced degrees, certifications, or specialized training programs can be a significant investment in your career. Many organizations encourage this type of learning by offering tuition reimbursement or partnering with educational institutions.

Online Learning Platforms: Platforms like Coursera, LinkedIn Learning, and Khan Academy offer courses on a vast range of subjects. These platforms are especially beneficial for learning at your own pace and tailoring your education to specific skills or interests.

Professional Workshops and Seminars: Participating in workshops and seminars provides opportunities not only for learning but also for networking. These events are often tailored to specific industries and can provide deep dives into niche areas, offering both practical skills and theoretical knowledge.

Reading and Research: Keeping up-to-date with the latest research, books, and articles in your field helps you stay informed about new concepts and industry trends. Dedicate time to read widely, from industry publications to blogs and white papers.

Peer Learning and Mentoring: Engaging with peers or finding a mentor can be an effective way to learn informally. This can be through structured mentoring programs or more casual peer learning setups. Both provide valuable insights and knowledge sharing based on real-world experiences.

Reflecting on the Role of Continuous Learning in Your Life

Incorporating continuous learning into your life is not just about professional development; it's about cultivating a mindset that values growth, adaptability, and curiosity. This learning mindset not only prepares you for the future of work but also enriches your personal life, providing a sense of achievement and fulfillment.

In conclusion, embracing continuous learning is essential for maintaining relevance and competitiveness in today's fast-paced work environment. It enables you to align your career trajectory with your personal growth and professional aspirations, ensuring that you not only adapt to changes but thrive amid them. By committing to lifelong learning, you ensure that your career is not just a series of jobs but a continuous journey of growth and satisfaction. This commitment is a key component of achieving and sustaining work-life equilibrium, where personal fulfillment and professional success are intertwined, each enriching the other.

Chapter 7: Overcoming Obstacles

Dealing with Job Burnout and Stress

In the realm of modern employment, job burnout and stress are not just common workplace issues—they are significant barriers to both personal well-being and professional productivity. Understanding how to effectively manage and mitigate these challenges is crucial for maintaining work-life equilibrium and ensuring long-term career satisfaction and success.

Understanding Job Burnout

Job burnout is a state of physical, emotional, or mental exhaustion combined with doubts about your competence and the value of your work. Often resulting from prolonged and intense job stress, burnout is characterized by three main dimensions:

- **Emotional Exhaustion**: Feeling drained, emotionally depleted, and unable to cope.
- **Depersonalization**: Developing a cynical and detached attitude toward one's job and colleagues.

- **Reduced Personal Accomplishment**: Experiencing feelings of incompetence and a lack of achievement and productivity.

Recognizing these signs early is key to addressing burnout before it becomes overwhelming.

Strategies for Managing Stress and Preventing Burnout

1. Setting Clear Boundaries: One of the most effective ways to prevent burnout is by setting and maintaining clear boundaries between work and personal life. This might involve specific cut-off times for work communications or designated work-free zones at home.

2. Time Management Skills: Effective time management is crucial for preventing burnout. Prioritizing tasks, breaking them down into manageable steps, and avoiding the trap of chronic multitasking can reduce stress and increase productivity.

3. Regular Breaks and Self-care: Integrating regular breaks into your workday can prevent fatigue and sustain concentration. Additionally, engaging in regular physical activity, ensuring adequate sleep, and pursuing hobbies and interests outside of work are vital for mental health and resilience.

4. Seek Professional Help When Needed: If stress and burnout symptoms persist, seeking help from a mental health professional can be essential. Therapists or counselors can provide strategies to cope with work stress effectively.

5. Workplace Wellness Programs: Engage in workplace wellness programs if available. These programs can include workshops, access to therapy, relaxation sessions, and activities that promote mental health.

The Role of Employers in Addressing Burnout

Progressive organizations recognize the impact of stress and burnout on employee productivity and overall health. As such, more companies are implementing supportive policies and programs:

- **Flexible Work Arrangements**: Allowing flexible hours or the option to work from home can significantly reduce stress for employees by helping them better manage personal and professional responsibilities.

- **Mental Health Support**: Providing resources such as employee assistance programs (EAPs), counseling services, and mental health days off.

- **Regular Check-Ins**: Creating a culture where managers regularly check in with their teams not just about tasks, but about their general well-being.

Cultivating a Resilient Mindset

Beyond organizational support, cultivating a personal resilience mindset is essential. This involves:

- **Adaptive Thinking**: Viewing challenges as opportunities for growth and learning rather than threats.

- **Emotional Regulation**: Developing skills to manage and respond to emotional distress effectively.

- **Support Networks**: Maintaining strong personal and professional networks that provide emotional and practical support.

Conclusion on Overcoming Job Burnout and Stress

Effectively dealing with job burnout and stress is not merely about finding quick fixes but about integrating strategies into your daily life that promote a sustainable work-life balance. It's about making consistent choices that prioritize your well-being, enabling you not just to function but to thrive both in and outside your professional environment. As we navigate through the complexities of modern careers, understanding and implementing these strategies becomes not just beneficial, but imperative for long-term success and happiness in both personal and professional realms. By fostering an environment—both internally and externally—that supports ongoing mental health and stress management, we lay the groundwork for a fulfilling and productive career life.

Navigating Career Transitions Smoothly

Career transitions, whether prompted by personal choice or external factors, are pivotal moments in one's professional journey. These transitions can range from switching industries or roles to climbing the corporate ladder or even starting a venture. Effectively managing these changes is crucial for maintaining not only career trajectory but also personal well-being and work-life equilibrium.

Understanding the Dynamics of Career Transitions

Career transitions involve more than just a change in job title or workplace; they often require a fundamental shift in identity and self-conception. As you embark on a new path, it's not uncommon to face challenges such as uncertainty, fear of the unknown, and the stress of new responsibilities. Recognizing and preparing for these emotional and practical challenges is the first step toward a successful transition.

Key Strategies for Smooth Transitions

1. Thorough Preparation: Before making a transition, it's essential to prepare both mentally and logistically. This preparation involves:

- **Research**: Understand the demands and expectations of the new role or industry. This might include the skills required, the culture of the industry, or the challenges you might face.
- **Skill Development**: If your transition requires new skills or knowledge, identify courses or training programs that can help you. This could involve formal education or more informal learning like workshops and seminars.

2. Strategic Networking: Networking plays a crucial role in successful career transitions. Building a robust network within your new industry can provide support, advice, and potential job leads. Techniques include:

- **Informational Interviews**: Reach out to professionals within the industry for informational interviews to gain insights and build relationships.

- **Professional Groups and Associations**: Join relevant groups and associations to meet like-minded professionals and stay updated on industry trends.

3. Financial Planning: Career transitions can sometimes lead to periods of reduced income, especially if the change involves starting a new business or a drastic industry shift. Adequate financial planning ensures that you can focus on your career development without undue stress about finances.

4. Personal Branding: As you transition, it's crucial to update your personal brand to reflect your new path. This includes your resume, LinkedIn profile, and even your personal pitch. Ensure that your new brand aligns with your career goals and the narratives you want to present to potential employers or collaborators.

5. Emotional Resilience: Developing emotional resilience is vital in navigating the uncertainties of career transitions. Techniques to enhance resilience include:

- **Mindfulness and Stress Management Practices**: Regular mindfulness exercises can help manage stress and maintain mental clarity.

- **Seeking Support**: Don't hesitate to seek support from friends, family, or professionals such as career coaches or counselors.

Leveraging Transitional Phases as Opportunities

View career transitions not just as necessary evils but as opportunities for growth and rejuvenation. Each transition holds the potential to propel your career to new heights if navigated thoughtfully:

- **Reflect on Your Career Path**: Use the transition period as a time to reflect on your career path. What have you learned so far? What are your future aspirations? How does this transition help you move towards those goals?
- **Embrace Learning**: With every new role comes the opportunity to learn something new. Embrace this aspect of your transition to enrich your professional and personal life.

Conclusion on Career Transitions

In conclusion, smoothly navigating career transitions involves a blend of practical strategies and personal development. By preparing adequately, networking strategically, managing finances wisely, updating your personal brand, and fostering emotional resilience, you can turn potential challenges into stepping stones for success. Remember, transitions are not just changes but chances to realign your career with your evolving personal and professional goals. They are pivotal moments that, when managed well, can enhance both your career satisfaction and your overall life equilibrium.

Chapter 8: Future Trends in Employment

Emerging Job Markets and Opportunities

As we forge ahead in an era of unprecedented change, the landscape of employment continues to evolve, shaped by technological advancements, shifting economic priorities, and global trends. For professionals navigating these changes, understanding emerging job markets and the opportunities they present is crucial for career planning and achieving work-life equilibrium. In this context, it's vital to explore sectors that are not only thriving but also offer potential for growth, innovation, and personal fulfillment.

Identifying Emerging Markets

Technology and Artificial Intelligence (AI): The tech industry continues to expand, with artificial intelligence leading the charge. AI is not just about programming or software development; it encompasses a variety of roles from ethical AI advisory positions to AI application in healthcare, finance, and creative industries. Careers in machine learning, robotics, and data science are particularly promising, requiring a blend of technical knowledge and creative problem-solving skills.

Renewable Energy and Sustainability: As global awareness of environmental issues grows, so does the demand for renewable energy solutions. This sector offers roles ranging from engineering and technical development to policy advocacy and green consultancy. Professionals in this field are not only contributing to economic growth but are also positively impacting planetary health.

Telemedicine and Digital Health: The healthcare industry is undergoing a digital transformation, accelerated by the pandemic. Telemedicine, health informatics, and biotechnology are significant areas where technology is being harnessed to improve patient care and health outcomes. Careers in this sector require not only medical knowledge but also skills in digital communication and data management.

E-commerce and Digital Marketing: The rise of online shopping has led to exponential growth in e-commerce and digital marketing. This sector demands a variety of skills from content creation and customer experience management to analytics and technical SEO expertise. As more businesses move online, the need for digital marketing professionals continues to grow.

Education Technology (EdTech): The field of education is experiencing transformative change with the integration of technology. This market offers opportunities in curriculum development, educational software design, online instruction, and more. EdTech professionals are at the forefront of shaping how educational content is delivered and consumed in the digital age.

Leveraging Opportunities in These Markets

Continuous Learning: To effectively tap into these emerging markets, continuous learning and skill adaptation are essential. Engaging in ongoing education and training programs can equip you with the necessary knowledge and skills to excel in these evolving fields.

Networking and Mentorship: Building a robust professional network and seeking mentorship can provide insights and opportunities within these industries. Participate in industry conferences, online seminars, and professional groups to connect with peers and leaders who can offer guidance and support.

Innovation and Adaptability: Embracing innovation and maintaining adaptability are key to thriving in emerging markets. Be open to new ideas and approaches, and be prepared to pivot your strategies as the market evolves.

Work-Life Integration: Consider how roles in these sectors align with your personal values and work-life balance goals. Many emerging industries offer flexibility in terms of remote work and unconventional working hours, which can be beneficial for maintaining equilibrium between personal and professional life.

Conclusion on Emerging Job Markets

As we look to the future, the intersection of technology, sustainability, and personal well-being defines the trajectory of emerging job markets. For those prepared to adapt and innovate, these fields offer not just new career opportunities but also the chance to be at the forefront of societal transformation. By understanding these dynamics and positioning oneself effectively, one can not only secure a place in these exciting new realms but also achieve a fulfilling and balanced professional life. Engaging with these opportunities allows for a career that is not just successful in traditional terms but is also enriching and aligned with broader life goals and values. This approach is not merely about adapting to change—it's about leading it.

Preparing for the Future of Work

As we stand on the brink of transformative changes in the workplace, driven by technological advancements, globalization, and shifting economic landscapes, preparing for the future of work is not just prudent—it's imperative. This preparation entails understanding the trends that are shaping tomorrow's job market and developing the skills and strategies to thrive in a dynamic professional environment. It's about being proactive rather than reactive, ensuring you are not only adaptable to change but can also anticipate and leverage it for career growth and personal fulfillment.

Analyzing Trends Shaping the Future of Work

Technological Integration: Technology continues to redefine the workplace, with AI, machine learning, and automation becoming integral in various industries. Understanding these technologies and their implications on job roles is crucial. For instance, while automation may eliminate some jobs, it also creates opportunities for new roles that require overseeing and integrating these technologies.

Remote Work and Flexibility: The shift towards remote work, accelerated by the pandemic, is likely to persist, altering not just where but how we work. This shift demands not only technological proficiency to manage digital workflows but also soft skills like self-discipline, communication, and time management to maintain productivity in a less structured environment.

Emphasis on Soft Skills: As technical tasks become increasingly automated, soft skills such as critical thinking, empathy, leadership, and adaptability will become more critical. These skills enable professionals to manage complex interpersonal dynamics, drive innovation, and lead effectively in a diverse global landscape.

Sustainability and Corporate Responsibility: Companies are increasingly judged not just on profits but on their impact on society and the environment. Careers focused on sustainability initiatives, corporate social responsibility, or ethical governance are expected to become more prevalent and influential.

Strategies to Equip Yourself for These Changes

Lifelong Learning: Commit to continuous education to keep pace with industry changes. This could mean formal education, such as degrees and certifications, or informal learning, like online courses, workshops, and webinars. Fields such as data analysis, digital marketing, and environmental science constantly evolve, requiring ongoing education.

Enhance Technological Literacy: No matter your field, increasing your comfort with technology is essential. Familiarize yourself with the latest tools and platforms relevant to your industry, from project management software to advanced analytical tools.

Develop a Global Mindset: As businesses operate on a global scale, understanding different cultures and how to communicate across cultural lines is invaluable. Learning new languages or studying international market trends can bolster your ability to work effectively in a globalized job market.

Networking and Collaboration: Build a robust professional network that extends beyond your current industry or role. Networking can provide insights into emerging industries and connect you with potential mentors who can guide your career development.

Adaptability and Resilience: Cultivate adaptability by embracing challenges as opportunities to learn and grow. Resilience will help you navigate setbacks or industry shifts more effectively, allowing you to rebound from challenges stronger and more prepared.

Reflecting on Your Career Path in the Context of Future Trends

As you look forward, it's beneficial to periodically assess your career path in the context of these evolving trends. Are your current role and industry likely to undergo significant changes? Are there opportunities you can seize now to position yourself advantageously for the future? This ongoing assessment can help ensure that your career does not just respond to changes but proactively aligns with the future trajectory of the workplace.

Conclusion on Preparing for the Future of Work

In conclusion, preparing for the future of work is about more than staying relevant—it's about being a step ahead. By understanding the trends shaping tomorrow's workplace and actively developing the necessary skills and strategies, you can not only secure your place in an evolving job market but also drive forward with confidence in your career and personal life. This proactive approach not only enhances your career resilience but also contributes to your overall life satisfaction, embodying true work-life equilibrium. By preparing today, you set the stage for success tomorrow, ensuring that your career journey is as fulfilling as it is successful.

Conclusion

Recap of Key Strategies for Work-Life Equilibrium

In this exploration of strategies essential for achieving work-life equilibrium, we've delved into various aspects of modern employment and personal development that are crucial for balancing a fulfilling career with a satisfying personal life. Here, we summarize the core strategies that can help individuals navigate the complexities of today's work environment while fostering personal growth and well-being.

Prioritizing Work-Life Integration

Understanding Work-Life Balance: It begins with a clear definition of what work-life balance means to you. Recognizing that this balance is not about splitting hours evenly between work and personal life, but about achieving fulfillment in both areas, is crucial.

Setting Boundaries: Effective work-life equilibrium requires firm boundaries—knowing when to work and when to step back and rejuvenate. It's about quality of work and quality of life, ensuring neither is compromised.

Embracing Effective Work Practices

Time Management: Mastering time management techniques such as prioritizing tasks, batching similar activities, and planning breaks can dramatically improve productivity and decrease stress. Tools like the Eisenhower Box or Pomodoro Technique can be instrumental in managing one's time efficiently.

Leveraging Technology: Utilizing technology—from sophisticated project management software to simple apps that help minimize distractions—can enhance efficiency and support a better work-life balance.

Cultivating Personal Growth

Continuous Learning: Staying relevant in your career through lifelong learning not only enhances job security but also enriches personal development. Engaging in regular educational activities, whether formal or informal, keeps you intellectually stimulated and professionally valuable.

Skills Development: As industries evolve, so must our skills. Proactively enhancing your skill set through courses, workshops, and self-study prepares you for future opportunities and challenges, making career transitions smoother and more successful.

Enhancing Job Satisfaction

Choosing the Right Role and Company: Understanding what makes a job fulfilling to you, whether it's the company culture, the type of work, or the industry itself, is key to long-term job satisfaction. Researching potential employers thoroughly and choosing roles that align with your personal values and professional aspirations can lead to greater satisfaction and success.

Networking: Building and maintaining a robust professional network provides support, fosters opportunities, and enhances career development. Networking should not only be seen as a professional activity but as a personal growth strategy that can offer new perspectives and ideas.

Maintaining Health and Well-being

Dealing with Stress and Preventing Burnout: Recognizing the signs of stress and burnout early on and taking proactive steps to address them is vital. This might involve seeking professional help, adjusting workloads, or incorporating mindfulness and relaxation techniques into your daily routine.

Physical and Mental Health: Regular physical activity, adequate sleep, and a balanced diet are fundamental for maintaining energy levels and mental clarity, both of which are critical for productivity and overall well-being.

Preparing for the Future

Anticipating Industry Changes: Staying informed about future trends and potential changes in your industry allows you to anticipate shifts and adapt accordingly. This proactive approach not only secures your place in an evolving job market but also positions you as a forward-thinking professional.

Embracing Flexibility and Adaptability: As the landscape of work continues to change, being flexible and adaptable becomes increasingly important. This means being open to changing how, when, and where you work, embracing remote and flexible working arrangements as they become more prevalent.

In conclusion, mastering work-life equilibrium is an ongoing process that requires dedication, self-awareness, and proactive strategy implementation. By applying these strategies, you can not only enhance your professional life but also enrich your personal life, ensuring that both are aligned and mutually supportive. This holistic approach to career and life planning is essential for anyone looking to thrive in today's fast-paced and ever-changing world.

Encouragement for Ongoing Growth and Satisfaction

As we navigate the complexities of modern careers and the elusive quest for work-life equilibrium, it is essential to recognize that the journey towards fulfilling personal and professional life is continuous and ever-evolving. The strategies and insights shared in this book are designed not merely as solutions to immediate challenges but as stepping stones towards long-term growth and satisfaction. Here, I offer further encouragement and guidance to continue your pursuit of a balanced and enriching life.

Embracing a Growth Mindset

The foundation of ongoing growth and satisfaction in both your career and personal life lies in adopting a **growth mindset**. This mindset, which views challenges as opportunities for development and embraces failures as lessons, is crucial for resilience and innovation. Cultivate this mindset by:

- **Seeking Feedback**: Regularly seek constructive feedback, not just from supervisors and mentors, but also from peers and subordinates. Use this feedback as a tool for self-improvement and career development.

- **Setting Learning Goals**: Continuously set personal and professional learning goals. Whether learning a new skill, enhancing existing abilities, or gaining deeper industry insight, these goals should challenge and motivate you.

Maintaining Work-Life Integration

Achieving work-life equilibrium is an ongoing process, influenced by changes in your personal circumstances, career transitions, and broader economic conditions. To maintain this balance:

- **Review and Adjust Regularly**: Regularly assess the state of your work-life balance. Be prepared to make adjustments to your schedules, commitments, and priorities as your personal and professional needs evolve.

- **Incorporate Flexibility**: Embrace flexibility in both your work and personal life. Flexibility can manifest in various forms, such as flexible working hours, telecommuting options, or flexible mindset towards changes and unexpected demands.

Investing in Relationships

Your relationships are crucial for personal satisfaction and can significantly influence your professional success. Invest time and energy in nurturing both personal and professional relationships:

- **Build Strong Support Systems**: Surround yourself with supportive family members, friends, and colleagues who encourage and motivate you. A robust support system can provide emotional stability and practical help during challenging times.

- **Engage in Community Building**: Whether it's your professional network or personal community, actively engage and contribute. Communities can offer a sense of belonging, increase your impact, and provide mutual support.

Prioritizing Health and Well-being

Never underestimate the importance of your physical and mental health in achieving ongoing growth and satisfaction:

- **Regular Physical Activity**: Incorporate regular exercise into your routine. Physical activity is not only crucial for health but also for mental clarity and emotional resilience.

- **Mindfulness and Mental Health**: Practice mindfulness, meditation, or other stress-reduction techniques. Consider professional help if you're facing persistent stress, anxiety, or depression.

Continuous Professional Development

In a rapidly changing world, continuous professional development is key to staying relevant and advancing in your career:

- **Stay Updated**: Keep abreast of industry trends, technological advancements, and shifts in the job market. This knowledge can help you anticipate changes and position yourself advantageously.
- **Embrace Lifelong Learning**: Dedicate yourself to lifelong learning. This commitment can be formal, such as pursuing higher education or certifications, or informal, such as participating in workshops, webinars, and other learning opportunities.

Conclusion

In conclusion, the path to work-life equilibrium is uniquely personal and continuously evolving. It requires a committed approach to self-improvement, an adaptable outlook, and a dedicated effort to maintain balance between professional aspirations and personal well-being. By embracing these strategies and maintaining a proactive stance towards growth and learning, you can not only achieve but also sustain a fulfilling career and a harmonious personal life. Let this book serve as your guide and inspiration as you forge ahead, balancing success in your career with richness in your personal life, ultimately leading to a holistic sense of satisfaction and achievement.

Summary

Introduction 3
   The Quest for Balance in Modern Careers 3
   Overview of Work-Life Equilibrium 6
      Setting Realistic Expectations 7
      The Role of Flexibility 7
      Technology as a Tool for Equilibrium 8
      Cultivating a Supportive Network 8
      Continuous Reflection and Adjustment 8
Chapter 1: Understanding Work-Life Balance 10
   Defining Work-Life Equilibrium 10
      The Fluidity of Equilibrium 11
      Personalization of Equilibrium 11
      Achieving Work-Life Equilibrium 11
      Tools and Strategies 12
      The Role of Employers 13
      Conclusion on Defining Work-Life Equilibrium 13
   The Evolution of Work Demands and Personal Life 14
      The Historical Context 14
      Technological Impact 15
      Societal Shifts 15
      The Millennial Influence 15
      Globalization and Economic Shifts 16
      The COVID-19 Pandemic 16

Looking Ahead 17
Chapter 2: The Psychology of Work Satisfaction 18
What Makes a Job Fulfilling? 18
    The Elements of Job Fulfillment 18
    Personal Alignment and Job Fit 20
    Creating Fulfillment in Any Job 20
    The Role of Employers in Enhancing Job Fulfillment 21
The Role of Motivation and Engagement 22
    Understanding Motivation 22
    The Spectrum of Engagement 23
    Fostering Motivation and Engagement 24
    The Impact of Motivation and Engagement 25
Chapter 3: Strategies for Achieving Work-Life Equilibrium 27
Prioritizing Tasks and Responsibilities 27
    Understanding the Value of Prioritization 27
    The Eisenhower Matrix: A Tool for Prioritization 28
    Strategies for Effective Task Prioritization 28
    The Role of Flexibility in Prioritization 29
    Maintaining a Long-term Perspective 30
    The Psychological Benefits of Prioritization 30
    Concluding Reflections on Prioritization 30
Effective Time Management Techniques 31
    Understanding Time Management 31
    Techniques for Enhancing Time Efficiency 32
    The Importance of Flexibility 34

Reflective Practice 34
Conclusion on Time Management 34
Chapter 4: The Impact of Workplace Culture 36
How Organizational Culture Influences Balance 36
Defining Organizational Culture 36
The Role of Leadership in Shaping Culture 37
Communication and Transparency 37
Policies that Promote Work-Life Equilibrium 37
Creating a Supportive Environment 38
Impact on Employee Retention and Attraction 39
Case Studies: Learning from the Best 39
Reflecting on Organizational Culture and Its Influence
 39
Case Studies: Companies Excelling in Employee Satisfaction 40
Google: Prioritizing Innovation and Well-being 41
Netflix: Flexibility and Responsibility 42
Patagonia: Integrating Values and Work 42
SAS: Emphasizing Employee Support and Balance 43
Reflecting on These Examples 44
Chapter 5: Tools and Technologies for Modern Job Hunters
 45
Leveraging Job Hunting Tools to Find the Right Fit 45
Comprehensive Understanding of Available Tools 45
Strategic Application of These Tools 47
Reflecting on the Impact 48

Online Platforms and Networking Strategies 49
Harnessing the Power of Professional Networking Sites 49
Utilizing Job Search Engines and Company Websites 50
Engaging in Industry Forums and Webinars 51
Building and Maintaining Your Digital Persona 52
Reflecting on the Role of Digital Tools in Modern Networking 52

Chapter 6: Personal Development for Career Advancement 54

Skills Building for Today and Tomorrow 54
The Importance of Skill Development 54
Identifying Key Areas for Skill Enhancement 55
Strategies for Effective Skill Building 55
Incorporating Technology in Skill Development 56
Reflective Practice and Continuous Feedback 57
Conclusion on Skills Building 57
The Importance of Continuous Learning 58
Why Continuous Learning Is Crucial 58
How to Engage in Continuous Learning 59
Reflecting on the Role of Continuous Learning in Your Life 61

Chapter 7: Overcoming Common Obstacles 62
Dealing with Job Burnout and Stress 62
Understanding Job Burnout 62
Strategies for Managing Stress and Preventing Burnout 63

- The Role of Employers in Addressing Burnout............64
- Cultivating a Resilient Mindset............65
- Conclusion on Overcoming Job Burnout and Stress....65
- Navigating Career Transitions Smoothly............66
  - Understanding the Dynamics of Career Transitions...66
  - Key Strategies for Smooth Transitions............67
  - Leveraging Transitional Phases as Opportunities........69
  - Conclusion on Career Transitions............69
- Chapter 8: Future Trends in Employment............71
  - Emerging Job Markets and Opportunities 71
    - Identifying Emerging Markets............71
    - Leveraging Opportunities in These Markets............73
    - Conclusion on Emerging Job Markets............74
  - Preparing for the Future of Work 75
    - Analyzing Trends Shaping the Future of Work............75
    - Strategies to Equip Yourself for These Changes............76
    - Reflecting on Your Career Path in the Context of Future Trends............78
    - Conclusion on Preparing for the Future of Work 78
- Conclusion 79
  - Recap of Key Strategies for Work-Life Equilibrium 79
    - Prioritizing Work-Life Integration 79
    - Embracing Effective Work Practices 80
    - Cultivating Personal Growth............80
    - Enhancing Job Satisfaction 81
    - Maintaining Health and Well-being............81

Preparing for the Future 82
Encouragement for Ongoing Growth and Satisfaction ... 83
    Embracing a Growth Mindset 83
    Maintaining Work-Life Integration 84
    Investing in Relationships 84
    Prioritizing Health and Well-being 85
    Continuous Professional Development 86
    Conclusion 86

www.ingramcontent.com/pod-product-compliance
Lightning Source LLC
Chambersburg PA
CBHW050232230526
45470CB00005B/1921